the LOVE & LIGHT

Words from the Angels

Gina M. Higgins

appublishing

Animal Dreaming Publishing
www.AnimalDreamingPublishing.com
A self-published title

The Book of Love & Light
A self-published title

ANIMAL DREAMING PUBLISHING
PO Box 5203 East Lismore NSW 2480
AUSTRALIA
Phone +61 2 6622 6147
www.AnimalDreamingPublishing.com
www.facebook.com/AnimalDreamingPublishing

First published in 2018
Copyright text © Gina M. Higgins
www.ginasdivineguidanceandhealing.com
Internal images © Gina M. Higgins

ISBN 978-0-6482455-2-0

This book is intended for spiritual and emotional guidance only. It is not intended to replace medical assistance or treatment.

Designed by Animal Dreaming Publishing

Printed in Australia

Dedications

To BJ and Amy, how can I not dedicate this to you? I truly wish you a life of love, joy and peace and all good things. A mother's love is unconditional. My hope is that this book may inspire you to see why I am who I am today and perhaps inspire you to live the life you desire with peace in your heart and to never be frightened of being YOU. I love you with everything in me.

Secondly, I dedicate this book to my team, my beloved Angels and guides who have changed my life in my knowing that they are there for me every day.

Contents

Acknowledgements

To all the beautiful people in my life that have encouraged me to step forward and let go of my fear in this amazing journey, I thank you sincerely as without you pushing me to fully believe in myself and what I have written, this book would never have reached publication.

So many amazing people, beginning with family: Mum, Dad, former husband and our children, brothers, sisters-in-law, nieces and nephews and of course so many awesome friends that have been my network of support as I transitioned into a new life. I simply want you all to know whether you have been in my life for many years or just a short while, you all mean so much to me and I appreciate you all for what you have brought to my life.

A big thank you to Bec for the gift of my first ever set of Angel Oracle cards that opened me up to acknowledging my true self and path. What a wonderful new way of 'being' came from starting to take notice of my inner guidance. It was all from writing a 'release' one day when pulling some cards for myself during a challenging time in my life that lead me to channel messages firstly for myself and then in the writing of this book.

To Dee, you truly have been my fairy godmother always there for me at any time and with you pushing me all the way to this point. I feel you have been an amazing strength behind getting me to where I am, so words are simply not enough. But THANK YOU my dear friend. I love you and appreciate you so very much.

Mum and Dad, you gave me life and so much more. The time I have spent with you in the last 12–18 months has meant so much to me and your support and encouragement means the world to me. I treasure this time we've shared going out, dancing, laughing and just having fun times together since my marriage ended. You have been my backbone in this time, and I'd have been lost without you and your awesome friends.

Wendy, Julie, Jen, Em. I cannot go without giving you a special mention also as you have been there for me with full understanding of every step I've taken in the last few years. You all came into my life through my work at some point in the last few years and yes some of you I may have been like your mentor, but you know that you came into my life for a reason and it was for us to help each other. You have all taught me so much along the way and I appreciate you girls so very much. Again, there are no words that can express my love and gratitude for you and what you have brought to my life. But, I know you can feel it from my heart and words are not really needed but thank you and I love you all.

Finally, to the many people that have been a part of my life who were an integral part of my growing and learning and teaching me things along the path of my journey to where I am today, irrespective of whether you are still a part of my life or not, you were in my life and I appreciate the lessons along the way.

Introduction

Many years ago, I began writing a book titled 'More to Life'. I had been running my own business and life was beginning to drag me down. As I write this, I feel a deep sorrow with the realisation that I had begun writing 'More to Life' because I'd lost my joy and spark. Life's stresses were draining my life force. My love and light were diminishing.

Even though I often expressed I was not depressed, it was whilst writing 'More to Life' that I began to realise that the reason I was writing my story was in fact that I was somewhat depressed! You see, I was becoming unwell. I was losing the light within. All my energy was draining from me. I was slowly losing the love inside me and was just going through the motions. Getting up, going to work, running the business, doing the shopping, dealing with family, dealing with life and its stresses.

Life had become mundane. Life had somewhat become lifeless. I became lifeless. I was living, breathing and loving my family. I was doing my job. But NOT living a life of love, joy or peace. But in all this I was also beginning to dream, dream of a better life.

One day I will finish my book, 'More to Life'. It's my story, from when I was around eighteen years of age to fifty, and how my journey led me to KNOW AND BELIEVE that there is more to life, and that the Angels and departed loved ones are by our sides helping us each and every day, guiding us to live a life of love, peace and joy. Through this journey and opening up to my spiritual path I discovered that I would write this book.

The Book of Love & Light is basic guidance from the Angels to help all live a more vibrant joyful life of peace. This book of LOVE is simply teaching all to release old energy and find ways to re-energise with the universal energy ... God's love and light.

During 2014, I found myself receiving messages through writing, and in these channelled messages my guides advised that I would put pen to paper to send the Angels' message to the masses to help people find their way to God's love and light again. Guiding all to love oneself, let go of fear, listen to intuition, learn to relax and live life with joy in their hearts to become the best that one can be.

In September 2014 they told me it was time to start writing, and so I did. Through the words they gave me the book unfolded. In December 2014 it was complete. However, I let fear hold me back. Fear of putting it out there and being judged. It's been quite a journey since then and a lot has transpired. I was guided to publish on many occasions. Although I knew this was best for all, and myself, I kept delaying it. *But it is time* and I now need to follow through with what they have entrusted me with. So, nearing the end of 2016, two years later, I was ready to follow through with what they asked and entrusted me to do. Now, in 2018, not quite another two years longer, comes the publication process of this book.

Chapter 1

Love Yourself— Give Thanks and Replenish

The Lord has spoken, and he says: 'Love yourself first'.

Within each and every one of you is a place that shines a light. This light needs energy. You are energy, but your source is drained on a daily basis and not many of you know how to, or to take the time to, replenish.

Loving and respecting yourself is a *must*. Universal energy is there to replenish at any time. You must listen to your self and take time out and give your heart and soul time to relax. Loving yourself first is a must in order to stay replenished and able to be the person of *love and light* that can shine and be the best you can be.

The first step in loving yourself is to always find something to be grateful for, and to show this gratefulness to God each and every day. When night falls, thank your God and Universe for your life and all the good things that have been offered to you. This step alone is fulfilling a requirement of recharging. Giving thanks and appreciation is a form of self-love and respect to God, our Universe and Angels.

When you take time each night to give thanks in prayer to your God, you will fill your heart with joy; it is automatic. Being grateful for the smallest of things will fill your heart and soul with joy and God will send his Angels to acknowledge your thanks with loving light. Light fills you in your entirety with the love and peace of universal energy to sustain you and energise you for a loving and peaceful life.

Even when you feel overwhelmed and life is pushing you and you feel downtrodden, rise up and be grateful. Trust yourself that you can and will always be able to find something to be grateful for. Love and respect yourself by acknowledging the things about yourself and your life that you appreciate.

As the days and nights turn into weeks and you continue to give thanks for all the small and big things, you will see more and more come to you to be grateful for. As you give thanks each night your list will grow. Love and light will fill you. You will begin to feel lighter, relaxed and at peace. Wonderful things will happen. As you respect yourself and your life by taking care of your own wellbeing and by showing thanks and appreciation for the life you have, the more you will begin to see that you have so much to be thankful for. You will then realise your hopes and dreams. In giving thanks by respecting and loving yourself and the life that you have, your God will give thanks and shower you with more to be thankful for.

So many loving people live a difficult and unsettled life. They easily fall deeper and deeper into a life filled with anguish and misery. They feel bothered and restless and hurt and let down. If only they knew that all it would take to turn their life around was to love themselves first, by respecting and honouring their wellbeing, and by being grateful for the good in life. The simplest of things can begin to turn an unsettled life around.

Be grateful for the friends in your life. The ones there for you, or the ones you enjoy spending time with. Love yourself enough to allow yourself the time to enjoy your friends.

Love and respect your body by replenishing it with healthy foods. Be grateful for the food that you enjoy. A simple piece of fruit can be appreciated! A piece of fruit for afternoon tea on a busy day is sweet, fresh, crisp or juicy and it re-energises you to get through the rest of the day. It can be as simple as this! You can be grateful for that delectable and nourishing food and the enjoyment it gave you. Love yourself enough to allow yourself to take time to enjoy that piece of fruit.

It can be that simple.

***

The Angels have shown me that it can be as simple as having time to sit outside. They've asked me to tell you that when I sold my business, I again found the pleasure of taking time to be outside in nature. I had time off after the sale of the business and although it was in fact a difficult time for many reasons, it was a blessed time. It was a time that I spent at home, reading my spiritual books and learning how to quieten my mind by sitting outside, enjoying fresh air and sunshine and listening to the breeze in the trees and the birds chirp and sing around me.

It was also a time I began to realise how much I had to be grateful for, and the time when I realised I needed to *love myself* enough to take time for me and how important it was to take care of myself and to *love myself* enough to know that it was okay to do so. It was a very important step in regaining my health.

I was always someone that tried to look on the bright side of things and be positive, but now I know there is more to do than be positive and that I need to express my gratitude to God and my Angels for what I have, and to be in the conscious moment to be able to appreciate the here and now and in doing so take time to *love and respect myself* enough to take good care of *me* and my wellbeing so that I could be the best that I could be.

I could list a myriad of things I am grateful for. I can tell you that being thankful will fill you with a loving feeling and that you will realise that by respecting and loving yourself and acknowledging what your life offers you, you will change your life.

***

So, start today. Tonight, when you lay your head on your pillow, give thanks for all the good in your life. Take a good look at yourself and acknowledge yourself. In return, feel the goodness in your heart and begin to love your life again.

And, love yourself.

Chapter 2

Love and Trust in Yourself

*With love in your being, great things
can be achieved.*

When the people of this life time realise that *love* is the answer to all, the world will begin to change.

As people trust themselves, they will relax and let themselves feel the love within. God has created one and all with love and light. As each soul begins their journey on earth they are filled with God's love and light to energise them for what lay ahead. Many are born to achieve great things, but first they have to find the love inside them to be able to spread their wings and become what they are meant to be.

It is sometimes a long and difficult journey, and a life of many ups and downs, on the path to enlightenment. You are all born with a plan that you have set in place, but it may take a lifetime before you come to the realisation that your higher self—the one you truly are; the one of love and light from God—is and always has been full of love.

Each person is capable of great things. When you trust yourself, trust your deepest most inner thoughts and instinct, you again fill with love and are able to move toward the life you are meant to have.

Many lose their way and in doing so simply forget they are filled with the love of God. At some point, usually when going through a very difficult time in their life, a realisation comes to them and they begin a new spiritual journey. Many have these spiritual moments through their lives. One day they begin to realise that if they trust within themselves, they can let God and the Angels hold onto all their worries and fears and can begin to feel lighter. By beginning to trust more in themselves and in God and the Angels, they begin to feel the love within them radiate once more.

Once the love begins to shine through them again, their life takes on a whole new meaning. Love and light from God fills their heart so that joy and peace fill their life. With trust comes more love of oneself. Feeling love and trust in oneself fills their soul with the light that they came from. Love and light engulfs them and soon a world of love, joy and peace is theirs.

As you continue the journey on this earthly plane, filled with love in your heart, you will see love everywhere. You will no longer see the negative that man creates. It's still there, but you can feel the love and light in you, so no longer will you hold hate, fear or anger when you notice or hear negative or low-energy people or occurrences around you. You will concentrate on filling your life with love and continue with a stress-free approach to life by trusting in yourself and allowing life to flow with love.

As mentioned in Chapter 1, if you say how grateful you are for the good in life—small and large—the love in that appreciation is received and bounced back to you. The more you begin to feel appreciation, the more you receive things to be appreciative of. Loving life and being surrounded with love and joyful things encourages more of the same.

When concentrating or focusing on negative, you lose sight of the joyful things and thus attract more low energy and more negative issues. Trust yourself to let go of all negative, fear-based and low-energy thoughts. When you trust in yourself and trust God and the Universe to take care of your needs, you can relax and breathe and begin to feel joy. Know that your Angels are always by your side. This should instil a sense of security. Trust yourself to be and to feel their presence. If you allow yourself to feel the love surrounding you each day and begin to acknow-ledge the radiating love around you, life will begin to shine.

Everyone has the capability to feel the presence of

their Angels. One just needs to take time to slow down, breathe deeply and feel the love and light that surrounds them.

Bringing joy and peace back into your life should be a priority. Simply trusting your instincts and feeling the love within you, lovingly placed there by God is the answer. Don't despair if you are at a point in your life where you feel that you have fallen into a black hole. Every human has a struggle at some point in their life on earth. Earth life can be difficult and challenging. The main challenge is in believing. Believing in yourself and listening intently to what you hear your higher self telling you. Trust it. Acknowledge it.

Believe that you put yourself here to live and learn certain things at this time. It is quite a journey and sometimes a journey that seems impossible. But, nothing is impossible.

I'M POSSIBLE.

Remember that! You are able to achieve whatever you put your mind to. Again, trust and believe in yourself.

In your darkest moments—when life seems unfair and you feel you have been tested one too many times—this is when you really must listen. Listen and hear your Angels talking to you, encouraging you to look past the heartache and pain that you have endured. Look past the negatives. Peek into the beautiful side of life. Believe. It is still always there. Love and light never leaves you. Stresses might bring a darkness that allows your ego and fear to cloud you and try to smother your love and light, but if you trust and let go of your fears and worries, love and light will shine through.

Remember to listen and trust your Angels and to trust yourself. Your higher self, your soul, is always trying to reach out to you and is there to defeat your ego—as long as you trust and believe in yourself, and not your ego!

Ego is what can cause you the most harm. Ego loves trickery. Ego lets fear step in. You all battle with your ego at some point and with most, ego wins nearly every time. It may take many years of highs and lows before you come to realise that the ego is your enemy.

When you come to this realisation and pay more attention to it, that is when you—your higher self and your soul—begins to win and truly fight back to allow the love and light within to shine through brightly. It is then that you see your true self!

Once you trust what you believe deep inside, you will feel lighter and stronger. You will gain courage that helps you brush away dark days and turn them into light-filled, joyful days. Feeling the love inside you radiates the light within, bringing peace into your world again. No longer will you fear anything. No longer fear that you don't deserve the good things you hope for. There will be no room for a fear of not having enough. You will become the master of your own destiny, a destiny that you chose.

All things are possible when you fill yourself with love and let God's light shine brightly within. All you have to do is *Trust*.

Trust God, trust the Universe and Angels and most importantly ...

Trust Yourself.

Chapter 3

The Gift of Love

When you were born, the gift of love was bestowed upon you. God filled your soul with all his love and energy for you to be ready for the journey your soul has chosen. You were born into this world through your vessel, your human body.

You choose your parents and awaited the day your human lifeform would enter the world. From that moment of choice, your soul is with that vessel until it is called back home.

God's energy is your life force. You are filled with his loving light. You begin your life journey with an energy that will sustain you throughout your time here on earth.

From the moment you are born, you have *free will*. It is this that allows you, as you grow, to choose your path along your way. Although you chose the path you wanted and needed for this time on earth to learn the lessons your soul requires as part of its spiritual growth long before you were born. However, from the moment you are born, you have no recollection of the path you chose before arriving, and with this you have free will at your hand.

Despite the gift of love that God has given you on your arrival, you may choose a long and difficult journey, and sometimes it is quite different to the path you initially intended on. With God's love inside you, your true life energy, you will have all good intention to succeed and fulfil the plans you put in place in your new life plan.

You will be given guidance from your Angels and guides throughout your time on earth. Even still, many somehow overlook the signs and messages from above. Many feel a presence but overlook it and are often too afraid to acknowledge the presence of these benevolent beings at their side throughout their life. If they would allow themself to openly feel the love inside them all would become clear.

God, our universal life force and energy, is always a part of us, filling us with his divine love and energising light. Getting lost along the way, so many beings feel crushed among the sorrows and hardships of their time on earth and in doing so, they lose their energy force and let it fall to dangerously low vibrations. They are living—But no longer alive! So many fall into the low vibrations and go about their lives dragging themselves along the way without ever becoming aware that they have the option and full potential to live a bright, love-filled and joyous life.

When God's Angels are able to finally reach them, and they begin to acknowledge and feel their presence, a new life force engulfs them. Their vibrations lift to become the light and love-filled being that they already are. The world around them changes as they begin to feel and see the beauty in front of them. God's love and light replenishes their lifeless body and their soul begins to sing.

Once God's love and light shines brightly again within, each human body rejoices again, and life turns around for them. They live the life of joy and peace and feel the love and light that is forever with them.

Life is meant to be joyous. There is so much to be grateful for. As each of you open your hearts and feel God's love and the Angels' presence, you can begin to truly love and honour yourself, your Universe, your beautiful planet and each other.

With open hearts and open eyes, you will begin to see the beauty that surrounds you. No longer looking at the negatives, no longer looking at or feeling the pain around you. Just breathing in the beauty that is life. Always acknowledging the wondrous glory of all that is bestowed upon you: the glory of God, your universal energy that is there for all to have and *be* and to enjoy.

This is the *gift of love and light.*

See the beauty that surrounds you. Breathe in the beauty that is life. Acknowledge the wondrous glory of all that is bestowed upon you: the glory of God, your universal energy that is there for all to have and be and to enjoy.

Chapter 4

The Truth

Jesus roamed the land spreading the word of God. Love and peace. He displayed many miracles and the people took note. They were compelled to act on the word of the Lord. They witnessed his miracles, and many were blessed with his healings.

To this day, it is all believed to be miraculous. Yes, what Jesus did *was* miraculous, but to set it straight, it is all achievable, and by all. Believe in your own miracles. God wants you to know that as life changes and human beings, souls on earth, come to the realisation that their world is made up of energy and God's infinite supply of love and light, they too will begin to see their own miracles come to pass.

Each passing year sees many millions drawn to the love and light and realisation of our life energy force.

A world of information is being brought forward. There are many books helping people learn and to open them to the reality of our world; helping them to understand that everything's made up of energy and that energy surrounds us. It fills us. Human beings are part of the life energy source, of God. We are all one. A part of what God created. Each and every soul that journeys to earth in a living body is made up of God's energy and filled with his love and light.

Along the path to enlightenment, each soul springs to life and feels God's love inside them. As they become more aware and open to this life energy force, they become aware that they have the power to move mountains and part seas. They realise that by being, they can create their own miracles.

You see, we Angels are always by your side, and God and his loving energy is always with you. You are part of the loving light and energy force; therefore, you are in charge of everything that happens through your own life force and your own free will.

Opening up to your life force and feeling alive with God's love and energy, you can grow and learn how to create your own miracles. The truth is, you all are capable of great things. Learning to live the life you are truly here for can open you up to creating those miracles.

Once you embark on a spiritual journey with God and his Angels, you will feel a shift in your life. You will become more aware of the presence—bit by bit—that surrounds you. You will feel the energy in everything that surrounds you.

It may be a steady journey, one that takes many dips, rises and falls, but it is a journey that will open your heart. You will feel the connection to your soul and the connection to *your* life force, to the Creator of all.

Feeling love and allowing your heart to open to all the good things around you will be the beginning of the miracles you can create.

God asks you, as his child, to feel the love inside; the love that he has filled you with. He will guide you to a beautiful existence of peace when you feel his love inside.

You will find the truth in the love inside you. God only asks that you open your heart and feel it. Look around you and take note of the beauty he has bestowed upon you. It's everywhere. It's there for you to feel and appreciate. Appreciating the beauty that surrounds you will simply fill you with his love.

It doesn't take much. Just open your heart and feel it. Open your eyes and see it. Trust that feeling and trust what you see. It's not all bad, you know. There *is* beauty everywhere. Once you begin to look and take notice of the wondrous beauty that life has to offer you, you will turn your life in a new direction.

It is as simple as this. God's love and light is surrounding you and within you. Begin now to notice the good around you. Find a way to let go of all your worries. Let go of any past and present pain. Let your fears go, and allow God and his Angels take care of them and thus, take care of you. Then begin to give thanks for all that you have and all that you know you can have. It's all there waiting. God has it all created, waiting. You just have to take notice and trust that you are capable of having the life you want and deserve.

God and his Angels are there always, beside you, with you, to guide you on your path to enlightenment. Feel their love and energy and accept their assistance. Begin to feel yourself re-energise. The simple truth about your journey is that all that you wished and hoped for can be yours.

God has his Angels with you doing his work and if you listen and allow, you can fulfil your life purpose. You decided long ago what you wanted from this life and with free will, you may have turned a few corners along the way that lead you in a slightly different direction. But now is the time to hear the words of the Angels and let God's love and light fill you again to bring you up and into the higher vibrational energy levels to allow you to achieve the greater good that you came here for.

Listen, learn, feel, love and trust your inner self to take you to the place of peace in your life that you so deserve.

Chapter 5

Pure Intention

It is now known that what you think, you create. Life is full of energy: it is everywhere and thoughts are a part of that energy. When life is throwing difficulty your way, it becomes all too easy to stay in a state of misery. The more you dwell on the misery, the more misery attaches to you.

The Angels have asked you to hear them as they explain to you that it is *your own intentions* that manifest and become the life that you lead. Put simply, for those of you that choose to always focus on pain and suffering and take note of all that you perceive to be bad in your life, you are simply placing the intention in the Universe that you are happy with the pain and suffering and the misery that you focus on.

You have all heard others speak positively, and you have at times taken note that there are people in the world, in your world, that clearly state their intention of correcting their life; their intention to live a more fulfilled, joyous and prosperous life. Once they put that intention in place in their minds, and they begin to focus on the good around them, the Universe works with them to manifest what they have asked for. Of course, there are some lessons in life that you came here to learn, and therefore, certain aspects of your life are a part of your original plan.

Begin by acknowledging the things in your life that you are grateful for. Each day, practice and take the time to give thanks to God and the Universe for the wonderful things bestowed upon you. This will fill your heart with love. Love in your heart is the greatest healer of all. Feeling love and appreciation for the good that surrounds you will help you to focus even more on good rather than the negative.

Those that choose to remain focused on negative will not turn their life around, not until the day they begin to let God's love and light enter them and remove the shadow of darkness that they have decided to live with.

Choice! It is yours. If you have the intention to change your life and begin to live a brighter, happier and prosperous life, make the choice today! Choose peace. Choose joy. Look around you and feel the energy that surrounds you. It is everywhere and you have an endless supply of pure and perfect energy. The choice is yours to make.

Do you choose to be grateful for trees and the birds or flowers blooming in your garden? Do you choose to see the love and joy in your children and hear the laughter in the playgrounds? Do you choose to be grateful that you have enough food on your plate and money to pay the bills? Do you still choose to be grateful for the food on your plate, although you may not have enough money at this present moment in time to pay *all* the bills? It all comes down to your choice. Only you can decide.

If, for some reason, you are having a difficult time, and your journey in life is testing you in a way that has lowered your energy and you are finding it increasingly more difficult to feel joy and smile ... then *now*, more than ever, it is important to look around you and take note of anything to be grateful for.

Be grateful that you have the support of loved ones. Or be grateful that you have your health. Those of you that are on your own or are battling illness, please still look around and find what is there for you to appreciate. If you open your heart and open your eyes, you will always find there is something to be grateful for. Be grateful for this opportunity to be living this life, to be learning in this life and to be able to *give* in this life.

You must live this life, learn from it and when you feel lost, open yourself up and feel your higher self speak to you. It will guide you to correcting the path and lead you to the path of enlightenment.

Simply put, you must hear your higher self trying to reach you in the darkest of days. Your higher self (your soul), along with God and the Angels, will want you to hear and take note of their guidance. They want you to feel the joy inside you come to life again.

Your intention from your higher self is to live the life of your true purpose, and once you shift that intention to your human mind to stay focused on all good and loving thoughts of joy and appreciation, more loving thoughts and joy will follow.

The more you practice and live a life of joy, love and appreciation, the less drama and the less stress and misery will be in your life.

Begin living the life you really want and deserve. Be compassionate, loving, caring, appreciative and positive. Endure the difficult and dark times by looking for the love and light of God.

Let the Angels guide you to a fulfilling and peaceful life. Make it your intention today to turn toward the life of love and light, joy and appreciation and a life where you no longer allow yourself to focus on negativity.

Be in the intention from this moment on so that you can live a wondrous life of peace and beauty. It is all in the *intention*. What is your intention?

Love. Light. Peace.

Chapter 6

Joy and Peace can be Yours

With every new day and every new breath, you have the opportunity to bring joy and peace to your life. By appreciating the beauty that surrounds you and by letting in and acknowledging the love and light that God has bestowed upon you, comes the peace that all mankind seeks.

Each and every human will search for peace at some point in their life. No matter where they are from, all are here on a similar journey, one leading them to the love of God and knowing that we are all one; all made from God's love.

Many children of God come to earth to celebrate. They finally learn the full extent of living a life of peace before entering eternity with God and the Angels in a world of pure love; a world of pure perfect energy and complete bliss and peace. Many lives can be lived before finding their way to this peace. Many lives of heartache, deception or pain can be experienced along the way to fully awakening.

During each time on earth as a being, lessons are learned. On returning to the eternal light of heaven, each will be debriefed and learn from their errors from that life. When they have fully healed, over many decades in earth time, they may choose to reincarnate and begin a new life on earth. Their intention on returning to earth life is to learn more and become the child of God, and love and practice the spiritual ways of their true and higher self. Once they awaken to this life of love and light and learn to express their love from God and the love within them, the peaceful and joyous life is the life they will live.

As more become aware of God's energy as a loving source, more will begin to share the joy of peaceful living. With every human that lives this peaceful loving life, God sends more love and light to share among them to help in spreading the word that his loving energy is the source of pure and gentle peace available to all.

God's Angels work closely with those already awakened, and with those who are on their spiritual journey. They guide them to the peaceful life they have longed for over their many lives. During this time of awakening and learning to feel God's presence with His everlasting loving energy and the presence of all Angels that surround all, humans become lighter and *Free*.

***

Learning to open up and work with the loving energy that is in and around us; sheds away the heaviness of our stressful lives that we have been living.

This energy is available to all, and God's Angels are there beside you all; helping and guiding you to fully open your hearts to this love and glorious energy. It is mostly during times of extreme hardship and pain or during life-threatening or near-death experiences that humans begin to take notice of the shift of energy around them.

It is in the darkest of days when life has taken its toll and one feels pushed beyond their limits of pain and frustration and full of disappointment that they begin to see, feel and hear the words of the Angels. The signs from the Angels are God's calling out to take notice that there is so much more available to each and every loving child sent to earth. It is during these times that messages are received. Messages come in many forms: You may hear something on television; or have a book given to you touching on spirituality; or simply read an article talking about energy; or hear the words spoken from another human crossing your path.

These messages are all divinely sent your way. You

were meant to hear, read or see that person or thing. It was the right time and it all happened just as it was meant to. God's Angels are always at work. Those little synchronicities are part of your journey. Divinely set in place so that you have the opportunity to hear, feel, see and take notice of the messages being sent to you.

As people start to open up and take notice of these signs, they become more aware of the other part of their life: the spiritual part, the side that most ignore.

For many, their awakening begins when they visit the Angels on the other side of the veil in a near-death experience. This changes their perspective, and on awakening they are almost fully enlightened and their true awakening has begun having seen for themselves the pure bliss that is available.

It is when life has thrown you all the hard times you can bear, that you begin to realise that what you've seen, read or heard about is beginning to make sense. For some, it is a long slow process. For many, it comes in waves of acknowledging there is more out there and more to themselves and the entire Universe. Then some slip back into the rut of life and go about living their life. Sometimes full on at a pace that they don't allow themselves to sit and truly relax and breathe in God's love and energy. It is during this wave that their energy gets depleted in rushing around living—that is, what they think is *living*.

They continue on their way. On the wave of rushing, stressing, working, playing and building a life of more wants and a life of less time for appreciation. They appreciate little that they have. Whilst working hard—or not working at all in some cases—they go about their daily rituals of running here and there or just lazing around and never taking time to look and see what is around them.

More and more the human kind just go about their business and daily life just working and thinking of what else they want. With the belief that with each want and receiving will give them the joy they seek. Sadly, they soon begin a cycle of living an existence of wanting more and not ever taking notice of what they already have. In this is born the materialistic world of ungratefulness.

There are those that during these 'waves' have times of acknowledging and appreciating their gifts from the Divine, God and the Angels. It is during these times that they awaken a little more and begin to take more notice of the signs. These signs from the Angels are to lead them to awaken their spiritual truth.

When the final wave is boarded, a true awakening arises. With this spiritual awakening, a true appreciation of all that is offered on earth is reached. One gets in touch with their higher self. The *true* person they really are. They have learned the lessons they came to learn. They have dealt with the hardships and pain that they needed to, and are now open to receiving God's love and light and filling their heart with the energy of the Universe.

It is with acknowledgement of this universal energy, God's source, that the shift begins.

Learning to live in the energy, feeling God's universal energy and pure love brings about a peace that fulfils their life's dreams. Once you all take notice and truly learn to live in the higher vibrations of love and pure blissful energy, your life becomes a magnet for the wonderful things you so lovingly deserve.

Feeling and acknowledging this energy is the beginning of living a peaceful and joyous life.

It is available to all.

Chapter 7

The People Around You

Children of God are always open to his love. Unfortunately during their passage in life they seem to forget that The Almighty is there: all day, every day.

Jesus, the son of God, came to teach the people about the love of God. They listened. But as the world grew into a materialistic world, people forgot. Greed became a part of life and although some still praised God and celebrated their faith, the love of God was lost among many.

More and more the world progressed toward an affection for *things*. This affection became an obsession and soon the world became full of people obsessed with working, making money: wanting more and *loving* less.

They loved less of what they had and still wanted more. Never satisfied with the things they had, they pushed forward and soon many became greedy and would jeopardise their love and what they already had achieved, just to gain more. They took bigger risks, just to gain more. Unjust behaviour and unfavourable actions became the norm for those that were becoming greedy. Ego stepped in and took over, telling them how great they would look with more and how clever they were in being able to deceive, cheat and gain more through unscrupulous accounts.

Then more people were becoming obsessed with money and objects. It was a growing world of greed and selfish people, wanting more of everything and never showing appreciation for what they already had, let alone the beauty of life itself and the world around them.

Our earth was being stripped of its beauty. Nature itself suffered. With progression, a world of magnificence was lost. Majestic forests and fields were torn down and stripped to build concrete blocks. It is okay to proceed, God says, but do it gently. Allow the beauty of nature to continue. Energy is all around you wherever you are but let there be a source through nature. Allow the trees and plants to grow wild and thus fill the earth with the energy from God. There must be a balance, he says.

Now with the new awakening and with the help of your Angels guiding you through your life to a realisation that you will always be taken care of, human life is shifting. Even those that have lived a greedy life of wanting and taking, are starting to take notice of those around them living more peaceful lives.

Life does not have to be so intense and painful. People whose existence revolves around working more and living less, wanting more and giving less, stressing more and relaxing less, smiling little and finding illness take over their bodies are slowly awakening to another realm of life, one that shifts them to see life in a completely different way.

People all around you have begun to take notice and ask questions. They question their own life first: 'Why am I doing this? There must be more to life!' And so it begins. The questioning opens their world to the spirituality that can change it all.

No-one wants to end up stressed and ill, and this is what generally happens. Through wanting more and living a life extended to greed, one becomes unhealthy in mind, body and spirit. It is a lesson that many learn, and regretfully, usually through a dramatic life changing event their eyes and heart open to a more spiritual life.

This is when the Angels send people that will help you along your spiritual journey. You don't have to look; they will be sent to you. They arrive in un-expected ways. You will receive messages and signs, although sometimes you won't see them.

The Angels make sure you receive guidance and will continue to send people and other signs to you to help you take notice until you begin to fathom what really is available to you.

These peaceful, loving people are all around you, and the little synchronicities in life that bring them to you can sometimes go unnoticed. All that matters is they reach you. When you are ready, and the time is right, you will take notice. All the information to help you understand and become more aware of your own spiritual growth becomes available to you.

It can be a long journey from living a life of wanting more and greed, living a life of working all hours that causes great stress, or a life of hardship and pain, to a life of spiritual beauty. No matter what your circumstances, God is there with you, part of you. His Angels beside you always, trying to reach you and re-energise you to bring you back in line with your true higher self.

Many people are in your life to help you along the way; some are there to teach you a lesson. You may be associated with someone that simply pushes you to achieve more and throws you deeper into despair in doing so. Perhaps you have been in contact with someone, be it through work or family, that drives you crazy in every way and you cannot tolerate their behaviour because you find it impulsive, abusive or irrational. Another might be a loved one that is rather cold and heartless and shows no affection, when all you want is to be loved, or maybe it is the opposite: your loved one smothers you with affection, but you desire some time out just for yourself.

If this happens, take a step back and see if you can evaluate why these people are in your life. It is with spiritual growth that you can visit these relationships and come to a realisation that they are for a reason. There is a lesson you can learn from these. *Everyone* around you has some importance to *you* and *your journey*. Even the big boss of the corporation you work for—who may be the greedy man that seems to have it all and you are unable to tolerate—will have a lesson for you. Stepping back during your spiritual growth, you'll be able to see that perhaps you once aspired to go all the way to the top and have it all; but if you've learned the lesson that he was there for, you now realise you don't want to be greedy, have all the greedy boss has whilst being uncaring and unhappy in doing so.

On the other hand, the same scenario might be quite the opposite. The lesson is that the big boss has achieved his dreams whilst remaining balanced and living a life of love. He has got to where he is without harming anyone and maintained a peaceful existence. He found a way to feel God's love and strive to do well whilst still living a joyful, caring and peaceful life. He is someone to look up to.

Not every person around is greedy or lazy or selfish or unmotivated. There is a whole world of people living God's way, enjoying the pure energy around them, living with God's and the Angels' love and light.

So, look around you and start to see these people. Take less notice of the *greed*, the *anger, resentment* and *fear* in the world. Let go of your own pain, fear and resentment. Let go of your worries. Look beyond all these things and live a life enjoying the beauty of the people who have found their way back into our universal love and energy. Learn from these people. You *can* have all that you desire and live the fulfilling life that you dream of once you let go and just *be*.

Be in this moment. Be with the people also that *shine brightly*. Be among those that live in the loving energy that surrounds you. These people around you will lead you to experiences that will open your heart. You will learn that there is a life waiting full of peace and joy.

People around you everywhere, just like you, are taking notice and want this life. You all have the capability, *remember*. You can make your life what you desire. It begins with believing in yourself, believing in God's universal energy that is everywhere and his love and light that can fill you and energise you.

Take a deep breath now and fill your lungs with his energy and move forward.

Chapter 8

Listening to Your Intuition

God has you all under his care. You were created with love and he wishes the best for you whilst on earth. He asks in return that you listen to your intuition, your higher self, your true self and soul trying to reach you. It is through your intuition that your soul and true self reaches you and attempts to pass on important messages and signs from above or near.

Your Angels are God's workers. They are nearby at all times and you are able to call upon them at anytime you feel the need. If your inner thoughts and feelings are guiding you to do, say, feel or think of anything—pay attention. Your Angels send you messages all the time through your own thoughts. So next time you think you might or should take a different route to work, but your ego or logic steps in and tries to tell you not to because it will add five minutes to the trip—pay attention and don't fight the thought. Do it. Take the other route! This is quite possibly your Angels steering you away from danger, or more than likely steering and guiding you to an alternate route, because they have a sign or message or someone you need to meet on the other route.

Listen always to your thoughts. On most occasions, your Angels have sent you this thought, this message, for a reason. Angels can get messages to you at any time so always be aware and pay attention to your intuition. You were blessed with this inner and most accurate way of feeling, and knowing what is right or wrong at any time, if you simply allow yourself to open up to it more freely.

All beings have at some time taken notice of this inner feeling of intuition, as well as fallen to the other side and ignored it. As you all would be aware, if you ignore that gut feeling things turn out with not the best outcome. Whereas, if you listen to that feeling—that intuitive feeling—and take the necessary action you were guided to take, you get a better outcome. It truly is a simple fact—intuition is there to help you. Listen to those feelings and thoughts and your Angels will help you in the right direction. Intuition will always guide you, so take notice of it at all times. It's very simple.

Trust that gut feeling. God blessed you with it so his Angels could reach you easily, and would be available to all no matter what stage of their spiritual journey they are at. Your higher self will thank you for listening to all intuitive feelings.

So, start today and practice taking more notice of your inner thoughts and feelings—the signs and messages from your true self and your Angel guides.

Practice taking more notice of your inner thoughts and trust your intuition.

Chapter 9

Releasing Your Fears

We Angels are here to carry your worries and fears. Trust them to us. We are able to hold them safely in order for you to remain peaceful.

Carrying worries and fear-based energy is of no use to you. In doing so, your energy and vibrations lower and your human body will become ill. It is of utmost importance to let go of all your worries and fears to the Angels. It may not feel as simple to do at first. However, once you realise that you have the capability to do so, you will find a peace within that will become a part of your everyday life.

Each time you become stressed, remind yourself that you most likely have no control of the particular stressful situation. You must simply allow yourself to remove these concerns by allowing the Angels to take care of all your worries so that you can clear your mind and allow yourself to relax, and can feel the love of God and your Angels re-energise you.

With allowing your Angels to hold onto your worries and all your fear, you will release the stress in your body and lift your energy and vibrations again to a joyous and loving state. Love, joy and peace is the state in which we all should be.

By holding onto fears and allowing stress to lower your vibrations, God's love becomes smothered with darkness. Letting go of the fears and worries to the Angels allows the loving light and energy to fill you again and bring you back into a light-filled energy.

The ego will always attempt to get you to take notice of all fears and any worries that will cause you stress; the ego does not want you to realise the potential of your higher self and the capabilities that your life holds. Trusting the Angels to take on your fears, releasing all worries to them, allows your higher self to concentrate on the true purpose of your being.

Without fear-based energy holding you down, your higher self is able to soar. Free of all worries and lower energies means that you will maintain a high vibration of love. In God's love and light, you will be able to remain focused on working toward your true life purpose. It is in this higher vibration of love that your soul is able to work with your higher self and talk to you through your intuition. In higher energy and working with your higher self you will be able to achieve more. The possibilities are endless.

Whilst the Angels are taking care of all your other concerns, you are able to get to work on manifesting your perfect life. Being in a state of love and higher vibration will allow you to move to a higher energy level and work with your Angels. The sooner you are able to work with your Angels and remain at a higher vibration, a place of love, the sooner you will be living a peaceful energised life of joy.

Start today and practice always. Any moment you feel yourself allowing fear to take over, or you are just worrying, please let go. Release those fears and all worries to your Angels and God and then open your life to peace and joy and the love and light of God.

Chapter 10

Breathing

Dear loved one, precious child of God. Please *breathe*!

Every living creature needs to breathe in oxygen to feel their life force generate within. You must sustain your human body with the breath. Too many forget to breathe. As strange as that may seem, it is fact.

Stress of life and allowing fear-based energies to consume you brings about an unbalanced energy and in doing so, causes this out of balance body to forget to breathe properly. During the stressful and dark periods of your life, you may not realise that in tensing your body, you in fact are momentarily holding your breath. This can occur thousands of times over the course of a day. This stress and auto-matic reaction of tensing muscles that causes your breathing muscle, your diaphragm, to stop the flow of air and life force energy readily entering your body.

Although your universal energy source is readily available to you, you will deplete your body of the much-needed energy source if you don't breathe in deeply. Breathing is of the utmost importance—that you all know. Without breath, your body is depleted of oxygen and your life force is gone. Your body will shut down. This is exactly why when you forget to breathe, and take in the oxygen your body requires, that your body becomes unwell. It is simple and so factual and many of you cannot fathom that people forget to breathe.

Let us explain more deeply.

God created you. He filled you with his love and light. He gave you plentiful energy and oxygen on the earthly plane to keep you sustained until your time to return home. He gave you free will. He does not force you in any way, whilst you are in your earthly body. It is your free will to live the life you have in the way you choose. He has his Angels working with you, along with your higher self (soul), guiding you at all times to live a healthful life and a loving life of service. But my loving children of God, you sometimes lose your way, forgetting that you are a blessed child of God, full of love.

Life slowly drains your energy as you let your ego take over and you get caught up in the materialistic world: running, working, wanting and taking on high doses of stress. Stress tenses your body, and as you run around in your crazy hectic stressful life with tensed muscles, you take fewer breaths. You take shallow breaths. You sometimes simply forget to breathe in deeply. Trust us, we know, we are watching and observing from close by and we attempt to remind you, but whilst ever you are stuck in the rut of your stressful life, you have blocked us and do not take much notice of our warning signs.

Fatigue sets in. Aching muscles and nausea. Then before you know it that stressed body that longs for slow deep relaxing breaths is screaming out for attention. If you ignore the signs we give and continue living the lifeless rut you are in, and continue to deprive your body of the real nourishing oxygen and energy intake that it requires, your body will let you know through illness. You are in fact manifesting illness so that your higher self will step forward and reach you before it's too late. Your higher self wants you to take notice. The Angels are there by your side, with you constantly, in an attempt to get you to awaken and hear your true self telling you that there is more to life.

There is more to living a stressful, unbalanced life. Once you listen and begin to take on board what your Angels are telling you, life will change. Hear their words. They speak to you in your thoughts. Your intuition saying that something is wrong is your higher self or Angels trying to reach you.

If you intuitively know that you are feeling unwell and need to cut all the toxic food and habits from your life, then listen and do so. We Angels will be with you to help you. The sooner you start working on slowing down your life and working on correcting those areas that are activating the stresses—which tense you and alter your breathing—the better you will become.

So, precious children of God, from this day on begin a new life. Begin today paying more attention to your breath. Breathe in deep gentle breaths to fill your lungs and *please* do not go about your hectic life forgetting to breathe.

Re-energise yourself with not only the oxygen you can breathe but with universal energy. Remember to also find time to go to a place of nature: a park, rainforest, river bed or lake; anywhere that you can take in the beauty of nature, and relax and *breathe*.

Chapter 11

Universal Energy

What is this universal energy? This is the question so many are asking. Yes, we know you have heard people talking of it, but what is it?

Let us tell you, dear children of God, God's love and light is your universal energy and God has created us all with it. Universal energy is everywhere and every person has access to it. Everything is made up of his love and light—of the energy of God.

Some call it the energy of the Universe, and some prefer to think of God as the universal energy. You are all correct. God is the universal energy and of course this equates to God being the energy of your Universe. Pure loving light is God's energy. God *is* pure loving light that shines on all he created and within all that he created. It is of God's pure loving energy that all on earth has been created.

You will hear of many of God's children working with his energy in varying ways. The most prominent way is that of healing. Healers are among you in varying capacities, and it is now a widespread knowledge that many are God's helpers and accessing his loving energy to heal others. Through many formats this practice is becoming more widespread. Not just in Eastern cultures, but throughout the western cultures as well. Not only through religious ceremony and prayer, but simply through awakened individuals, on their spiritual path who have come to the realisation that they are one of God's helpers and able to heal others in a spiritual way as well as with physical and psychological ailments. These individuals become attuned and responsive to the universal energy and are able to act as a conduit and call on God's energy to come through them and pass through their hands to those they are working on.

Though there are many forms of energy healing being utilised, it would seem that Reiki and Reconnective Energy Healing seem to be the most commonly spoken of at this point in time, although some also carry out healings without any attunements or official trainings and simply work through direct prayer with God. Profoundly, God's workers are able to source his energy through prayer and call on him to assist with healing.

Energy healing is healing with universal energy—healing with God's loving energy. It is with great sadness that we hear so many religions doubt this and in fact give it a Satan-type mythology. We are everywhere and we do assure you all that working with any energy healing modalities are of God's love. There is no darkness about healing with God's universal energy. These remarks come from fear-based beliefs.

All we ask is that *all* kind remain focused on God's loving light letting go of those fear-based mis-conceptions. Please be of the understanding that there is but *one Creator*. Many choose to worship our Creator through different names, however, we assure you, irrespective of what your chosen name is for the worshipped—God, Buddha, Krishna, Jehovah, The Tao and the like—all religions, all faiths, do worship the *same* God of love and light. You may name it whatever you choose, but it is the *one* Creator—the one universal energy of love and light that you are all from.

Chapter 12

Choosing the Right Path

We are always beside you. Angels are there with you every day guiding you and assisting you along the path of your life on earth. With our help, you can fulfil your true life purpose, but you must be open and able to hear our words and take note of our guidance.

It is with us walking with you along the path of life that you learn and move forward to the awakening of your true spirituality. Along the long, tedious road of awakening that each soul is destined to learn the lessons they came to earth to learn. Some, along this path, may take the wrong turn and the lessons are lost. Without their intuitive thoughts resonating and waking them up to their higher self, these lost lessons can steer them in the wrong direction and onto a path of what seems like damnation and into the depths of darkness. Lost along the way, sometimes frightened of their dark and lifeless persona, they are unable to find their light within. Their higher self continues reaching out but to no avail, with them ending up going deeper and further into their lost journey whilst their guidance continually attempts to steer them back to the light of God.

These souls are working hard to recover; however, many remain on a journey heading in the wrong direction. These people may turn to crime, horrible acts of abuse and self-abuse. Some turn to fear, sorrow and depressive behaviour which can also turn to addictions of all kinds: drugs, alcohol, self-harm, lifeless humans also forgetting to maintain their earthly body with love or to caress it with healthful food and practices.

Many turn to greed and lack of respect for others. A journey full of anger, fear, greed and abuse lowers one's love and energy. It could continue to spiral until they become so unwell and their life force is so depleted that they leave the earthly plane without having learned their life lessons.

However, many on this journey can and do turn away from the direction of pain and anguish, fear and despair and greed and lust. They awaken to the life they are meant to be living. This is why we have so many Earth Angels among you. They are there to help those that are lost on their path. An Earth Angel coming into your life at the right time can steer you empathetically in the right direction. Gently guiding you and teaching you of the new ways you need to become aware of. With love and guidance from your Angels and God you too can be led to those in need or those in need are led to you.

Whilst they may have endured times of hardship on earth, they are very real and human and able to understand and help those in need. Angels teach all that need a little help to awaken, and teach them to learn about the higher self and their own spirituality.

God's love and light is always there. It is available to all, but not those who follow the path of condemnation, and close themselves off and do not want to hear their own inner thoughts and intuitive guidance, let alone their guidance from Angels. These lost children of God sometimes stay in the darkness and therefore will need great healing and counselling when they leave earth. When their time is up and they return home to God, their guides and Guardian Angels will work with them and work through the errors of their ways on earth. They do this so that they will be aware of what lessons they missed in order to address them on their return at a later time. But many are able to awaken in time and turn their life into the path and direction that they had chosen for their soul purpose for their time on earth before this happens.

Tragically, it is through major crisis in life that the realisation arrives that they need to alter their path. It is through this dark period that the love and light from God can shine through at its brightest and in its fullest glory. We know you have taken note of others that have fallen and whilst at their lowest point, they change within themselves and become the person that they truly were meant to be. A new life arises. A person of love and integrity shines through from the dark. Others still lost on their path may shun those that awaken to God's love, whilst others will learn from these awakened souls and find their way. Sadly, these people cannot see or understand that these loving souls have let go of all their fear, anger and lower energies and are now true to themselves and living a loving peaceful life, full of joy instead of pain and anguish.

Thankfully through these people that have chosen their new path—the path of spirituality, love and light, peace and joy—others learn of their own spiritual being. Many follow and learn from the newly awakened. A world is evolving of true love and peace. As more become aware that they can turn their lives around by believing and trusting in themselves, God and the Angels, a world of peaceful loving beings are available to teach more lost beings how to find their way to God's love and way of life. A life of love and light.

Chapter 13

Pure Love and Affection

Angels are of pure love. Having a relationship with your Angels will fill your world—your life—with pure affection.

There is no greater joy than the loving affection you receive from your Angels and God. Building your relationship with the Angels and God will fill a void that you may have felt in your heart for some time. It is with the greatest joy that we hear your prayers and feel your love when you open yourself to us.

Through your journey of awakening, we guide you and listen to you when you call for our help. You just need to think about us and we are there. We hear your every thought and at any moment can be there to comfort you or protect you. It is your free will to go through your life in whichever fashion you choose, therefore we do not interfere. However, in cases of emergencies, we can step in for your protection.

You can always trust that we offer you compassion, love, affection and respect at all times, and it is with the highest of love and gratitude that we receive your love in return. We feel deep love on awakening. Once you make the choice to allow us to be a part of your life and openly and clearly invite us in, we are there for you to receive our purest love and affection at all times. We are at your beck and call as your personal protectors and for personal guidance.

All it takes is to open yourself to your intuition. We reach you and guide you through your intuitive thoughts and feelings. The more you open up to your spiritual world, the more you can feel and sense us with you. We can communicate with you in many ways. For some it is easy to hear, feel and even see us, generally through the third eye (mind's eye).

Being in a place of pure love and peace will open you up even more. For some it can be a long journey to awaken their spiritual senses. For others, they simply hold on to their spiritual senses and psychic abilities from childhood. Some children remain in the pure place of love and peace and forever allow themselves to be open to the spiritual world and remain in a state of being a part of their Angels' lives. They continue their relationship with the spiritual world and most go on to be well known mediums and psychics and spiritual healers. Others know and sense that there is more around them but may not fully allow themselves to open up to this other world, the world of beautiful, peaceful Angel friends and God.

On doing so, the long journey of fully awakening leads them to the place of bliss; a life of peace and joy with all their needs met by remaining in a happy, positive and loving state. By remaining in this state, living a life of no negativity and no fear, allows them to bring forward all their desires and full potential. They become their true selves, working in a place of love to complete their full life purpose. They find it increasingly easier to remain in a state of love and in tune with their higher self. God's love and light shines even brighter through them, and with the help of their Angels' guidance and love, they share the love with others and teach more and more about the possibilities of a greater and more fulfilling, enriching life filled with pure love and affection that re-energises their soul.

Go for long walks on the beach or in nature. Feel the sun on your face, or the wind in your hair.

Chapter 14

Releasing Old Energy

Dance under the stars, sway to the breeze in the trees and feel the rhythm of the music you play. No need to feel any inhibitions. Just go with the joy that you feel as you move to the sounds that feel good to your heart. These are simple and effective ways to release old and lower energy. We cannot express this to you in any simpler terms. You do not have to carry toxic energy and weigh yourself down with old, stale negative and fear-based energies that can and will make you ill. Release all old energies to the Universe.

We tell you it can be as simple as moving, and as simple as feeling the love inside you come to the surface. Let all your worries go and help yourself re-energise by allowing yourself to release anything that holds you on a lower energy base. Movement releases stress and therefore moves all stale energies that you have allowed to attach to your body and soul.

Call upon your Angels to assist you with releasing the old energies that have clogged your system. You do not need to store old ways, old harsh energies, nor hold onto any fear from past situations or current situations that cause you stress. We have spoken with you about letting go of your fears and about asking us for help. We are there *always* and will assist you if you call. At this moment in time we are with you and we are helping you understand that you have the power within yourself to change it all, with or without our help.

To feel good, start moving. Get up and go out and enjoy nature. The Creator has it all there for you to enjoy. You have all you need at your disposal. You have beautiful surroundings to feel the glorious energy that sustains you and the planet earth. Go and enjoy them and feel lighter. Feel its love surrounding you.

Now feel all the energy that is at your disposal. Utilise it. If you are feeling weighed down and stress is becoming a factor of your life, take time to *move*. There are so many ways for you to move. Dancing, singing and music are wonderful expressions. Enjoy the movement and expression and let yourself become one with it.

Exercise is another thing. Go for long walks on the beach or in nature. Feel the sun on your face, or the wind in your hair. Take a stroll in the moonlight. So very simple to exercise and take care of yourself to replenish your energy system and soul.

The potential to remain well is as simple as this. Just moving and releasing the old energy and allowing the new energy to keep you sustained.

Break away from the stress holding you down. Let it all go and allow us to take care of your worries. Nothing gives us more joy than to see God's beloved children happy, healthy and enjoying their life. We promise you this. Please hear our words and move to release old stale energies. Do not allow fear and negativity deplete you. It is within your power to feel well and happy, be content with life and feel God's eternal love and light.

If for some reason you are unable to move to release old energy, call upon your Angels to assist. Arch-Angel Michael is the almighty helper and protector who will come to you at any time. Just call upon him and his mighty helpers, his band of mercy workers. ArchAngel Michael will come the instant you call on him. Being omnipresent, he is able to be anywhere at any time. Ask him to cut all etheric cords of fear and lower energies that are attached to you. Ask him and his band of mercy workers to vacuum away all the lower and dark energies you have absorbed, either past or present. He can remove old energies for you and it is as simple as asking him to do so. Call on him now:

ArchAngel Michael, I call upon you now. Please cut all cords of fear-based lower and negative energies that I may have attached to me. Assist me to remove all old stale energy, those fear-based, negative energies, that I have absorbed within my humanly body. Please clear away all old energies from around and within me at this time.

Take a deep breath as this powerful ArchAngel goes about clearing all the old energy from your body. You may shiver as this work is carried out. Relax and allow him to do his work. Give thanks for his assistance and take in his loving energy now.

It is of no importance to us what your circumstances are. All we wish to do is be available if you call for our help. We do not judge. Our highest intention is to assist you to live your life in a healthy and happy way in order to fulfil your intentions for your time on earth. We are here to quietly offer guidance. For this we ask you to be open and ready to hear and receive our messages. So, by beginning to move and freely releasing your fears and worries to us, you become lighter. It is time to slow down, remove excess stress from your life and whilst doing so, begin to move and release all old, stale energy so that you can begin living a life filled with pure loving energy and the brightest of loving light that is readily available to you.

Move today. Walk. Dance. Sing. Exercise. Clear that stale energy and take note of the way you begin to feel. This is an important step to feeling God's love around you. Becoming lighter is the opening for us to come and reach you.

Chapter 15

Joy and Happiness

We Angels are our brightest when we see God's children happy. We are here now to tell you it is okay to dance, sing and play. It is our greatest pleasure to see you enjoying yourself.

We do not expect you to live your life completely at our beck and call. You are not expected to be in a state of meditation at all times. Therefore, we are happy for you to listen to other music that brings you joy. Yes, it is true that your vibrations are on a higher level when you are in a state of relaxation, especially whilst listening to Angelic harmonic or meditative pure energy music as we are able to reach you more easily at these times.

However, we *do not* judge you if you choose to listen to other music played from your favourite musicians.

Nothing gives us more joy than to see you smiling, relaxed and releasing your stress. Music does this, and we acknowledge that moving to music is a form of stress relief as spoken about in the previous chapter. We feel that there must be equilibrium to all. Please know that it is okay to thump along to your favourite music as we know it brings you joy. You are on this earthly plane and living through some difficult times so please do make time to enjoy whatever it is that gives you joy and happiness during this time.

Meet up with friends and take time to relax. It is not all about work. It is okay to take time out to enjoy life. Go on that break. Visit family away. Go to the beach or bushwalking. Go see that band. Have a party too. Buy that boat. Go fishing. Go dancing. Play that game. Enjoy your sports. You are there to live. Being happy and relaxed will help you live it freely and with less stress. Less stress means you become lighter, and being lighter lets you feel God's loving, bright energy. Feeling lighter opens you to the spiritual world around you.

Whilst you enjoy life and release your worries and stress, we are there by your side waiting for your calls offering quiet guidance. When you become lighter and in a place of pure joy and peace, you begin to take more notice of our softly spoken guidance. Your inner self begins to listen intuitively to your own higher self and to our messages through thoughts.

So please, God's children, live your life fully and do what it is in pure love and light that brings you joy. We love to see you happy and safe.

Chapter 16

Live Your Life as it Should Be

We have spoken to you about people around you who are having a significant effect on how you live your life and have spoken about how some end up on the wrong path.

Do not fret, dear children, all will be okay. You will always be accepted back into God's heavenly home of love and light at the end of your days on earth. There is no condemnation. You will be with us in this heavenly bliss once you leave your earthly body.

God welcomes you all home in the end. You do not have to live a life of fear, fearing that you will not return. There is just a glorious heaven on the other side of the earthly veil, always ready to take you home in all its glory, and for you to live in eternal peace.

Please do not think that the many paths that you take on earth are ever wrong and taking you away from God forever. This simply is not true. You can always come back to God and his loving Angels. He assures you of peaceful eternity and every path you take will always lead you to him.

Many of his children make choices through their own free will that leaves them with an emptiness and sometimes darkness that drains their true life force of God's love and light. Some return home having not been able to correct their paths, and find themselves with many lessons unrealised. On returning to God's care, the Angels counsel these children so that they come to see their ways on earth that have left them empty and drained. Many of these children of God that have swayed and become out of balance will heal and choose to return to earth at another time to learn and experience what they missed on earth in their previous incarnation.

It is with great joy that we are now seeing many of you on earth turning your inner self to the light and love of God. A new awakening has been the path for many over these last decades. Slowly, there comes forward a true spiritual awakening among you. The true path of living your life of love and peace has been realised by many now. This pleases us immensely, and we are finding that many are now living their life true to their higher good and true purpose, and in doing so, giving us access to reaching them more clearly and readily each day.

A life of peace and harmony with no stress or anger is creating a lighter and brighter energy for you all. Vibrating in a higher space and creating loving energy is drawing others to you. As others are drawn to those already awakened, they become more curious to why these awakened beings are filled with such joy and radiating a loving, bright energy. They question why these radiant beings seem to have it all: a relaxed, loving lifestyle full of abundance and joy. These loving, bright beings are most likely also some of God's special Angels sent to earth to enlighten the world.

Through the beautiful Earth Angels, God spreads his message across the earth. More and more begin to follow these loving souls and learn from them. Through this we now see a whole lot of beautiful beings becoming unblocked and cleared of stale energy, and free themselves and step on to the path of their true spiritual being. This leads them to the life they are meant to be living—the life of God's pure love and pure white light and energy.

This spiritual awakening brings a life of joy, peace and abundance. This life is available to all. We have explained through these writings that on releasing your fears and all worries to us, you will lighten your load and will in turn re-energise. Once you release all stale energy and let God's Angels fill you again with his loving light, you can become the person you are meant to be. With God's love and light in every part of your being, there will be no room for negativity and fear. You can and will become all that you wish to be.

With this my loving children, we say to you. We are here for you at all times. We love you in every aspect of your true being. We can be called upon to heal you and to lead you to the life that you are meant to be living. Let us bring joy and peace into your life. We are ready and waiting to fill you again with God's love and light.

And so it can be … And so it is.

About the Author

Gina is a 52-year-old mother of two adult children living in the sapphire city of Inverell, NSW. A psychic medium and Reiki Master, she has been running a small a home-based business over the last few years helping those that need assistance in life. Intuitive healing and reiki sessions or spiritual and guidance readings incorporating assertiveness coaching, spiritual and holistic counselling and stress management offer her clients the ability to move forward in life with more ease.

Working from a place of love is the answer, and finding peace helps everything to fall into place. Gina's no stranger to a life of stress and disharmony but has always put forward a happy positive attitude to get her to where she is now. Her spiritual journey over recent years has given her the courage to step out and into being more authentic. Her faith in what she believes has helped her improve her own wellbeing and be of service to help those that need help to find peace and healing on their journey.

If you want to learn more about Gina visit her website: ginasdivineguidanceandhealing.com or follow her on Facebook at:
www.facebook.com/angelcardreadingsbygina

Believe in God's universal energy that is everywhere and his love and light that can fill you and energise you. Take a deep breath and fill your lungs with his energy.